CULTURE IN ACTION

Digital Music

A REVOLUTION IN MUSIC

Claire Throp

Raintree

Chicago, Illinois

www.heinemannraintree.com
Visit our website to find out more information about Heinemann-Raintree books.

To order:
☎ Phone 888-454-2279
🖥 Visit www.heinemannraintree.com to browse our catalog and order online.

Edited by Louise Galpine and Diyan Leake
Designed by Victoria Allen
Original illustrations © Capstone Global Library Ltd 2011
Illustrated by Randy Schirz
Picture research by Hannah Taylor

Originated by Capstone Global Library Ltd
Printed in and bound in China by CTPS

14 13 12 11 10
10 9 8 7 6 5 4 3 2 1

Library of Congress Cataloging-in-Publication Data
Throp, Claire.
  Digital music : a revolution in music / Claire Throp.
    p. cm. -- (Culture in action)
  Includes bibliographical references and index.
  ISBN 978-1-4109-3915-9 (hc)
  1. Sound recording industry--History--Juvenile literature. I. Title.
  ML3790.C666 2011
  781.49--dc22
                        2009052581

Acknowledgments
The author and publishers are grateful to the following for permission to reproduce copyright material: Alamy Images pp. 7 (© ClassicStock), 8 (© Index Stock), 24 (© Jeffrey Blackler); Corbis pp. 17 (Reuters/Kin Cheung), 22 (LA Daily News/Gene Blevins); Getty Images pp. 4 (bilderlounge/Lisa Penn), 6 (Imagno), 9 (AFP/Yoshikazu Tsuno), 10 (Time Life Pictures/Ted Thai), 11 (AFP/John MacDougall), 16 (Newsmakers/Alex Wong), 26 (AFP/Yoshikazu Tsuno); Photolibrary pp. 12 (Corbis), 14 (Raymond Forbes), 18 (Herve De Gueltzl), 19 (Baron Baron); Reuters p. 13 (Rick Wilking); Rex Features pp. 20, 23 (Dan Talson), 27 (Lehtikuva OY).

Cover photograph of a person listening to an MP3 player reproduced with permission of Getty Images (Taxi/Yoichi Nagata).

We would like to thank Patrick Allen and Jackie Murphy for their invaluable help in the preparation of this book.

Every effort has been made to contact copyright holders of any material reproduced in this book. Any omissions will be rectified in subsequent printings if notice is given to the publisher.

Disclaimer
All the Internet addresses (URLs) given in this book were valid at the time of going to press. However, due to the dynamic nature of the Internet, some addresses may have changed, or sites may have changed or ceased to exist since publication. While the author and publisher regret any inconvenience this may cause readers, no responsibility for any such changes can be accepted by either the author or the publisher.

Author
Claire Throp is an experienced author and editor of books for young people. A big fan of music, she can often be found listening to tracks on her MP3 player.

Literacy consultant
Jackie Murphy is Director of Arts at the Center of Teaching and Learning, Northeastern Illinois University. She works with teachers, artists, and school leaders internationally.

Expert
Patrick Allen is an award-winning author and music educator, whose work as an Advanced Skills Teacher of Music takes him into schools, colleges, and universities.

Contents

Some words are printed in bold, **like this**. You can find out what they mean by looking in the glossary on page 30.

What Is Digital Music?

Do you listen to CDs or an MP3 player? Do you **stream** or download music from the Internet? If so, you listen to **digital music**.

Analog versus digital

Analog music may be stored in a **format** such as a **vinyl** record or a **cassette** tape. Over time, the quality of music stored in analog format gets worse and worse. For example, the grooves in a vinyl record will wear out after repeated playing. Digital music is stored in a format such as an MP3 file. A digital recording is not only clearer than analog in the first place—it also stays that way no matter how many times it is played.

What type of music do you enjoy listening to?

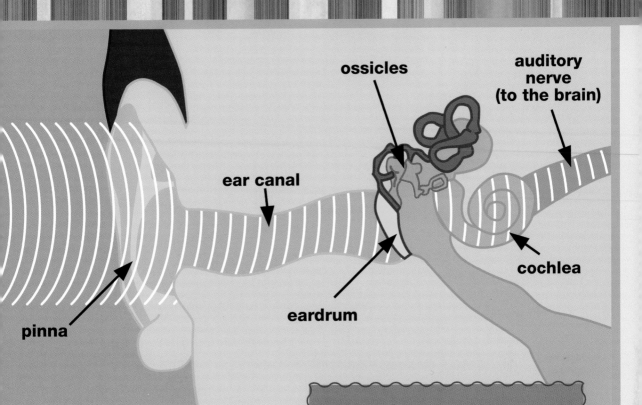

ossicles

auditory nerve (to the brain)

ear canal

pinna

eardrum

cochlea

New technology

Technology has changed the way that people have listened to music over the years. It is improving all the time. This means there are not only new ways to listen to music, but also new ways to make music. You can download computer programs from the Internet and create your own songs. You can even set up your own radio station!

Hearing sounds

When something vibrates (moves back and forth very quickly), it moves the air. This creates sound waves. The pinna catches the sound waves, and they go through the ear canal to the eardrum. Tiny bones called ossicles vibrate, carrying the sound to the cochlea, which is filled with fluid. The fluid moves and pushes the sound along nerves toward the brain. The brain makes sense of the signals, and we hear the sound.

The History of Music and Sound

In the late 1800s the first sound recordings were made. Thomas Edison recorded "Mary Had a Little Lamb" on a phonograph. A needle recorded the sound into a groove on a foil-covered cylinder (tube). Then the machine played back the sound through a horn. It was only possible to record two minutes of sound on that first phonograph.

In 1887 Emile Berliner created the gramophone. Sound was now recorded onto discs made of glass. They were similar to the **vinyl** (plastic) records that are still sold today. Each disc could play four minutes of recorded sound. It was easy to make copies of these recordings, which meant that many people could buy them. Discs were cheaper than cylinders, and they became popular.

Thomas Edison

Thomas Edison was born in 1847 in Ohio. He was the youngest of seven children. He was mainly schooled at home by his mother. He was interested in science and always wanted to know how things worked. He became an inventor. In 1877 he invented the phonograph (right). This was the first machine that could record and play back sound. Edison is also famous for inventing the electric light bulb. He died in 1931 at the age of 84.

Radio

In 1906 the first radio broadcast was made to ships in the Atlantic Ocean. This was the work of Canadian inventor Reginald Fessenden. The program included speech and music, much like the radio we know today. However, it was not until the 1920s that the idea really took off.

In the first half of the 1900s, a popular pastime was for people to gather around their radio to listen to their favorite programs. This was a time before television!

Recording to tape

Magnetic tape was developed in 1928. After some improvements to the quality of the tape, a tape recorder was invented called the Magnetophon. This type of recording was also known as reel-to-reel tape recording. The tape on one reel would wind onto another reel during recording and play back. It meant that radio programs, for example, no longer had to be performed live. They could be recorded and then played at a later date.

Everything gets smaller

A transistor is a device that makes electrical signals stronger. Transistors were developed in 1947. This meant that electronic machines could be a lot smaller than they were before. The first transistor radio was sold in 1954. What was special about this was that the transistor radio was **portable**. It was much bigger than the players we are used to, but it could still be carried around.

Until the 1980s, using reel-to-reel tape was the main way to record music.

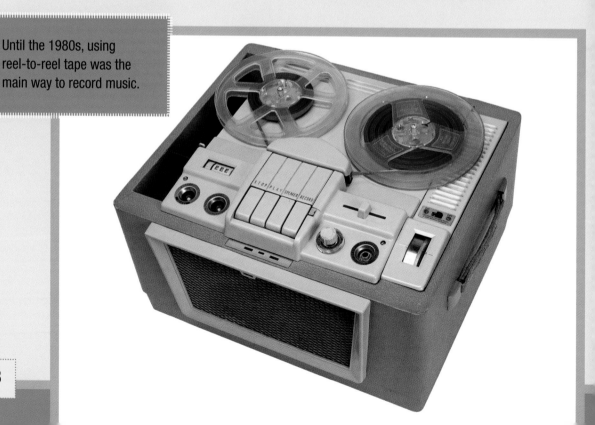

The small **cassette** tapes that can still be played today were first sold in 1963 by a Dutch company. The tape was enclosed in a plastic case, which meant it was less likely to be damaged. Cassette tapes were soon very popular.

In 1979 a portable cassette player called the Walkman was first sold in Japan. Ten years later, more than 50 million had been sold around the world. However, it also led to the awareness that listening to music on a Walkman with the volume too high can lead to deafness.

In the 1980s, the Walkman changed people's listening habits. Suddenly, people could listen to music on headphones as they went about their daily lives.

The Digital Revolution

In 1982 the first compact disc (CD) was sold in Japan. It was originally created to record classical music. A piece of classical music usually lasts a lot longer than rock or pop songs. CDs offered a lot more recording time than a record or a **cassette**. The sound was clearer and CDs were less likely to be damaged. It was also easy to skip a song or find a particular section of a song. With cassettes, fast forwarding to the next song could take some time. CDs and CD players were considered to be luxury items at first because they were expensive to buy. Gradually they became cheaper and were soon more popular than cassettes or records.

In 1996 CDs that included multimedia files were released. They were known as enhanced CDs because they did not just include music. If they were played on a computer, extra features such as a video or animation might appear.

The quality of the sound and the amount of music that could be recorded onto a CD were big selling points.

People who worked in the music **industry** had to learn new skills when digital recordings became popular.

Digital recording

Music is often recorded in a building called a studio, using equipment including a computer with recording **software**. However, the wide availability of computers means that musicians do not have to hire an expensive studio. As long as musicians have a computer, recording software, and some basic equipment, they can record music at home.

You can listen to music on a music player or even a cell phone.

Downloading music

The real change in the way people use and listen to music came with the invention of the MPEG-1 Audio Layer 3 **format** (more commonly known as MP3), and the development of **broadband** Internet. Since the late 1980s, scientists had been developing the **technology** to **compress** files so that they could be run on a computer. When computer files are compressed, it means they are made smaller. Usually a compressed song takes up roughly one-tenth of the space a CD-quality song would take up on a computer. Smaller files can be transferred easily across the Internet or between devices.

One of the most popular ways of listening to music today is to download it from the Internet. Music can be downloaded into different compressed formats. The most common format is MP3, but there are others, including Waveform audio (WAV) and Windows media audio (WMA). Advanced audio coding (AAC) is a format that was designed to replace MP3. It is an improved way of compressing files, and the sound quality appears the same as that of CDs. Not all of these formats can be used on all players, however.

Sansa slotMusic players have music preloaded onto MicroSD memory cards. These cards can be used in **portable** music players and cell phones.

Internet safety tips

When you download music from the Internet, remember these safety rules:
- Don't go on the Internet without a parent or caregiver's supervision.
- Don't give out personal details online.
- Be careful when opening attachments if you don't know who sent them.

Fast Internet connections

The Internet was very slow when it was first introduced. Broadband connections are much faster, and speeds are improving all the time. It might once have taken an hour to download a song, but it can now be done in minutes or seconds. This makes it much easier for people to download music. It also means that listening to **streamed** music is much easier.

Advantages of downloading

One of the best things about downloading music is that songs can be bought individually. Not everybody wants to buy a whole album. What makes it even better is that you get the music right away. Some people even suggest that downloading may be the most environmentally friendly way to buy music because you can do it from home and there is no packaging or postage required.

Prices of portable music players are falling. This means that more people can afford to buy them. Cell phones often have music players, too.

Design a cover for your music player

Design a cover to protect your music player or phone. You could ask an adult to help you make it.

Steps to follow:

1. Decide what colors and patterns you are going to use for your cover. While you are working you can listen to your music player to get ideas. See if you can match the design to your favorite type of music. If you like pop music, for example, you could have different colored bubble shapes on your cover. If you like rock, maybe you could try a design with a flash of lightning.

2. Choose your material. Thick material will be better for protecting your music player.

3. Measure your player or phone to make sure you use a big enough piece of material. Ask an adult to help you cut out the material and any shapes for your pattern. Be careful with the scissors!

4. You could use fabric glue to stick the pieces together or ask an adult to help you sew the main pieces of material together.

5. Decorate your cover with glitter, sequins, or shapes made from different colored materials.

15

How Digital Music Affected the Music Industry

In 1999 a U.S. teenager named Shawn Fanning wrote a piece of computer **software**. He used the software to set up a website called napster.com. This allowed people from all over the world to share the music they had stored on their computers. Other people could then download it to their computer for free. It meant that people could listen to music that they had not actually paid for. It was known as **file sharing**, or P2P (person-to-person) networking.

Shawn Fanning of Napster stood trial in court in 2000.

Record companies

Record companies are groups of people who are in charge of a number of different singers or groups. They ask artists to sign a written agreement called a **contract**. In return they record the artist's music and do their best to sell it.

The record companies were not pleased about Napster because it meant that fewer people bought CDs. If people could download music for free, why would they pay for it? This meant lower **profits** for the companies. The Recording **Industry** Association of America stood up for the record companies and **sued** Napster for breaking **copyright** laws. This was because Napster was providing other people's music without permission.

The record companies argued that if artists do not receive payment for their music, they will suffer. People working for record companies will also suffer, and perhaps even lose their jobs, if companies do not make enough profits. Shawn Fanning lost the court case and Napster was shut down. Napster has since reopened, but it is now a service that you pay for. People today continue to use many other illegal file-sharing sites that have sprung up.

These recording artists from Hong Kong are protesting against illegal downloading in April 2004.

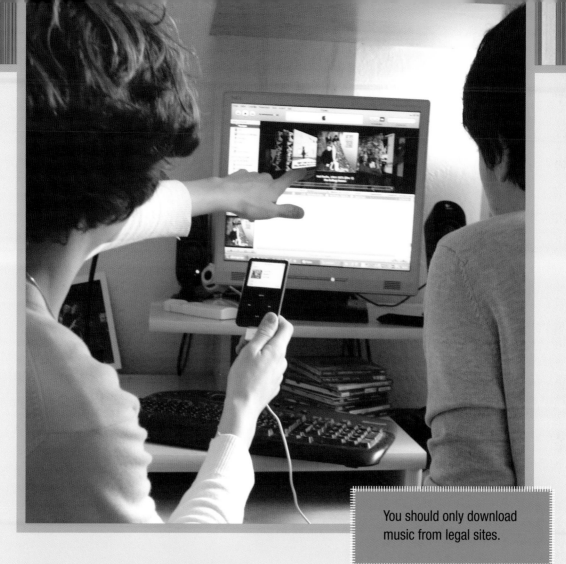

You should only download music from legal sites.

Is file sharing stealing?

Some people think that using file-sharing websites is wrong because artists will not be paid for their work. The argument is that it is the same as stealing. You would not have a snack in a restaurant and walk out without paying. Why should music be any different?

Some people think that file sharing helps the artists because their music is heard by as many people as possible. They may also believe that the only ones affected will be the big record companies. However, the money that artists would receive from the sale of every CD or **legal** download is also lost.

The danger of file sharing

File sharing means that anyone with an Internet connection can use it to download music from other people's computers. The music you can download from these sites may have a virus (harmful computer code) attached to it that can badly damage your computer. Also, music from P2P sites may not be very good quality.

Digital rights management

Have you ever downloaded music from iTunes? The website once used a digital rights management (DRM) system. DRM limited the number of computers that a song could be played on to five. When the music file was downloaded, it included information about that computer. It noted how many times the file had been transferred to other computers. The music would not play on a computer that was not authorized (allowed to play the music).

Portable music players are so small you can fit them in your pocket.

How much would you pay?

In 2007 the British rock band Radiohead decided to make its new album, called *In Rainbows*, available on the Internet. The band said its fans could download it for whatever price they wanted to pay. The recording industry was worried. Radiohead is a popular band that could sell a lot of CDs. Radiohead was not the only band to attempt such a change. It was another example of a threat to traditional music selling.

Today, many artists offer **streaming** files on their websites. Often the music cannot be downloaded. However, musicians hope that by making some of their music available for people to listen to for free, people will then buy it. Some bands also provide streaming videos on websites such as YouTube.

This photo shows Radiohead performing in 2009, playing songs from their album *In Rainbows*. The average amount that their fans paid to download the album was $6.

Set up playlists

Do you have a special occasion coming up such as a birthday party? If so, you could make a **playlist**.

Steps to follow:

1. With a friend or family member, decide what kind of music would work best for the occasion. Think about:
- what event is taking place
- how many people will be there and how old they are
- where it will be held
- whether there will be dancing.

For example, for a birthday party, think about the age of the person and what type of music he or she likes.

2. Ask an adult if you can use the computer. If you don't have a computer, you can write your list on a piece of paper.

3. Imagine what will happen at the party, and set each tune down in order to match each event. For example, when the cake is being cut, you could have quiet music in the background.

Trends in Digital Music

The music **industry** is going through a major change. Online sales are becoming increasingly important. Musicians can now reach fans more directly by creating their own websites. There are companies with the aim of marketing (selling the music of) bands that have decided not to get a recording **contract**. Record companies are realizing that they have to change.

Artists might think about not signing a record contract because they can earn more money by selling their music themselves. One CD costs very little to make, but the artist receives only about one-tenth of what it is sold for. Most people would pay at least that if they were just to download the album off the Internet.

Special shows introduce new **technology** to the world, including new ways of listening to music. The Sansa slotMusic player (see page 13) was introduced at the 2009 Consumer Electronics show in Las Vegas, Nevada, shown here.

Ringtones

One of the biggest areas for **digital music** sales is cell phone ringtones. Some artists are recording special ringtones at the same time as recording their albums.

Vinyl records

Vinyl records lost popularity when **cassettes** became more common, but some people still like listening to them. Digital music can also be marketed through selling vinyl records. Some records include a code that allows the buyer to download a digital version. They get both the vinyl and the digital versions for the price of one.

Vinyl records are popular with DJs.

Digital Radio

Another way to hear music is to listen to digital audio broadcasting (DAB) radio. This is radio that broadcasts music and other programs as a digital signal. A special radio is needed to listen to the digital sounds. There are many digital radio stations, which means you are bound to be able to find one that plays your favorite music.

Internet radio (or **streaming** radio) is also popular. There are so many choices that you can even listen to stations that only play music from the 1980s! Listening online also means you can hear radio based in other countries.

HD radio

The latest **technology** allows radio to be broadcast in high definition (HD). This means that the sound will be clearer than ever before. All that is needed is a radio that can receive the HD broadcasts.

There is no hiss when you listen to digital radio. There are more stations, and some DAB radios can even pause and record music to play back later.

Write a new song

Have you ever wanted to write your own song? Try this with a friend!

Steps to follow:

1. Listen to the radio, either a DAB radio or online. There are many stations to choose from, especially online. Just search the term "online radio" and there should be lots of results.

2. One of you should try jumping from one station to the next to pick up phrases from different songs. Practice by listening to songs that you both know well.

3. Ask your friend to repeat the phrase and then write it down. Write each phrase on a separate piece of paper.

4. Try mixing the pieces of paper so that the words make sense. It doesn't matter if you don't copy the phrase exactly. It's just to help you create a song to perform.

5. Think about the kind of song you want to finish up with. Perhaps it could be hip-hop, pop, or heavy metal.

6. Now sing or rap the new songs to each other!

The Future of Digital Music

Music fans have changed the way they buy and listen to music as a result of digital **technology**. The big record companies now do more to promote the sale of digital albums rather than digital singles. These album downloads come with digital album booklets similar to those that come with records or CDs.

Subscription services are becoming more popular. This is when people pay a certain amount of money and can download a number of songs each month. Interactive radio is another idea that has taken off. This would allow you to choose which music to listen to as you are listening to the radio. It will probably be a few years before it happens, but it is possible that the CD will gradually disappear.

This is the "Rolly," an MP3 player that has motion-sensing chips in it like a Wii does. You can change the volume by simply rolling the player with your finger.

Unfortunately, it is very difficult to control what happens over the Internet. This means that **file sharing** will probably not go away, particularly as technology improves.

Exciting times

It is difficult to know what will happen to music in the future. New music players will be developed and Internet connections will get faster. The only thing we can be sure of is that technology will continue to improve. This means that the ways we can listen to music will continue to change, too.

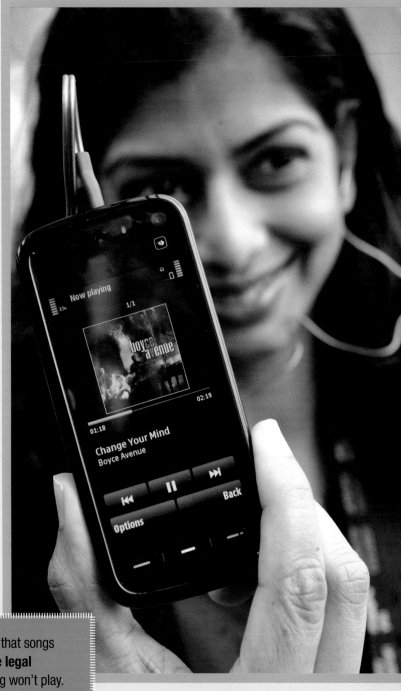

There are plans to check that songs played on cell phones are **legal** purchases. If not, the song won't play.

Timeline

1877	Thomas Edison makes the first sound recording on the Edison Phonograph
1887	Emile Berliner invents the gramophone
1890–1897	Guglielmo Marconi works on experiments that eventually lead to the invention of the radio
1901	First radio signals are transmitted from Cornwall in the United Kingdom to Newfoundland in Canada
1916	Radios have tuners to allow people to listen to more than one station
1930s	Period known as the "golden age" of radio
1939–1945	World War II
1947	The transistor is developed
1954	The first transistor radio is sold
	Elvis Presley releases his first single
1962	The Beatles release their first single
1963	First compact **cassettes** are sold
1973	The first cell phone is made. It is much larger than the ones we have today.
1979	The Sony Walkman, the first personal stereo, is launched in Tokyo, Japan
1982	The CD is introduced in Japan

1984	The Apple Mac computer is first sold
1987	German scientists develop a way to shrink video files to run on computers
1989	The World Wide Web is invented
1990s	Cell phones and the Internet become more and more popular
1998	MP3 players for listening to downloaded music appear
1999	Shawn Fanning writes a computer program that allows people to access and share their music on the Internet on napster.com
2000	The Napster court case takes place
2001	The first iPod is sold
2004	An official download chart is first produced
2005	Nine Inch Nails releases *With Teeth* on MySpace
2007	The first iPhone is sold
	Radiohead releases *In Rainbows* online and lets its fans decide how much they want to pay for it
2009	The Featured Artists Coalition calls for a strict rule for people who download music illegally, reducing their **broadband** capability so that they would not be able to download music
	"Low" by Flo Rida becomes the best-selling digitally downloaded song of the decade, with 5.2 million downloads

Glossary

analog music music that includes the electronic noise that is removed from digitally recorded music. The quality of music recorded in analog format gets worse every time it is played. Analog music cannot be understood by computers unless it is first changed into digital code (numbers). This means it is harder to alter after it has been recorded.

broadband high-speed Internet connection

cassette tape that runs from one reel to another inside a plastic case. The tape has sound recorded onto it.

compress squeeze data (music) so that it takes up less space on the computer or music player it is stored on

contract written agreement. A recording contract is made between an artist and a record company to set out what has been agreed upon, such as how many albums the artist will make for the record company.

copyright set of laws that prevents people from copying the original work, in this case a song, of another person without permission

digital music music that has been broken down into code (numbers) so that it can be understood by a computer or other digital devices. The sound quality is usually a lot better than an analog recording.

file sharing downloading files from the Internet without paying for them

format type of file that a sound recording is available in—for example, MP3

industry groups of people, called companies, who make and sell something. The music industry makes, records, sells, and arranges performances of music.

legal allowed by the law of a country

playlist set of songs chosen and put in a particular order for a particular event

portable can be carried around. MP3 players and cell phones are portable.

profit amount of money that is left after all costs have been paid

software computer program

stream listen to sound or music as it is being downloaded from the Internet. Streamed music is not owned by the person listening to it.

sue start a claim in a court of law against another person or group of people

technology use of tools and power to invent new machines and to make machines work

vinyl plastic. Vinyl records are round and flat and music is recorded onto them.

Find Out More

Books

Allman, Toney. *Downloading Music* (Ripped from the Headlines series). Yankton, S.D.: Erickson, 2007.

Mack, Jim. *Hip Hop* (Culture in Action series). Chicago: Raintree, 2010.

Miles, Liz. *Making a Recording* (Culture in Action series). Chicago: Raintree, 2010.

Sturm, Jeanne. *MP3 Players* (Let's Explore Technology Communications series). Vero Beach, Fla.: Rourke, 2009.

Websites

www.wiredkids.org/wiredkids_org.html
The WiredKids website has games and activities to remind you how to use the Internet safely.

http://radio.real.com/children?pageid=radio.home-ns&pageregion=nav
This site has links to radio stations online.

Index